W9-AUZ-217

Ancient Innovations

The Technology of the Aztecs

Naomi V. McCullough

Cavendish Square

New York

Published in 2017 by Cavendish Square Publishing, LLC
243 5th Avenue, Suite 136, New York, NY 10016

Library of Congress Cataloging-in-Publication Data

Names: McCullough, Naomi V., author.
Title: The technology of the Aztecs / Naomi V. McCullough.
Description: New York : Cavendish Square Publishing, [2017] | Series: Ancient innovations |
Includes bibliographical references and index.
Identifiers: LCCN 2016021836 (print) | LCCN 2016022616 (ebook) | ISBN 9781502622396 (library bound) |
ISBN 9781502622402 (E-book)
Subjects: LCSH: Technology--Mexico--History--Juvenile literature. | Aztecs--History--Juvenile literature. |
Aztecs--Civilization--Juvenile literature. | Mexico--Civilization--Juvenile literature. |
Mexico--History--Juvenile literature.
Classification: LCC F1219.76.M37 M37 2017 (print) | LCC F1219.76.M37 (ebook) | DDC 972.01--dc23
LC record available at https://lccn.loc.gov/2016021836

Editorial Director: David McNamara
Editor: Kristen Susienka
Copy Editor: Nathan Heidelberger
Associate Art Director: Amy Greenan
Designer: Joseph Macri
Production Coordinator: Karol Szymczuk
Photo Research: J8 Media

Contents

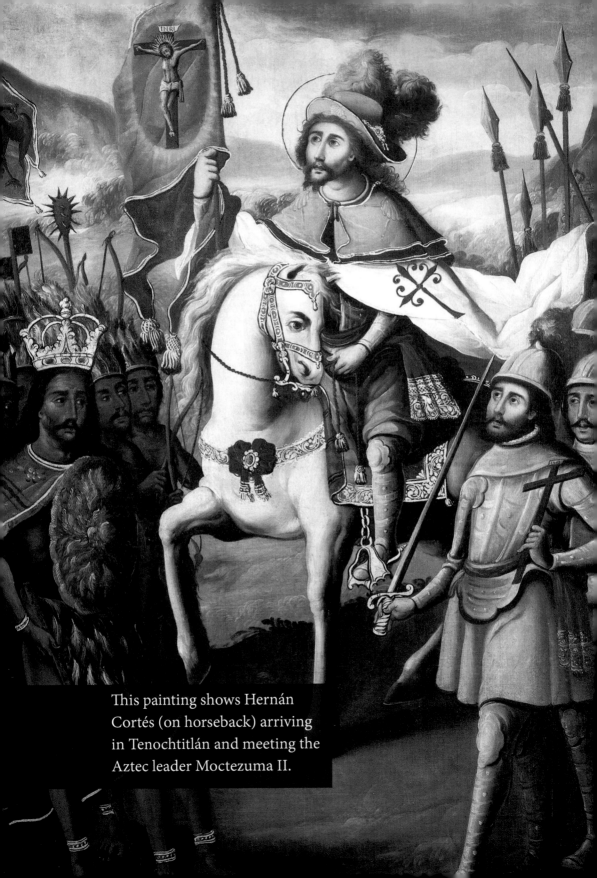

This painting shows Hernán Cortés (on horseback) arriving in Tenochtitlán and meeting the Aztec leader Moctezuma II.

Chapter One

An Empire Evolves

B efore the arrival of the Spanish in the 1500s, **Mesoamerica** was a land untouched by outside influence. Its landscape was full of dense forest, unique wildlife, and prosperous civilizations of people. The men and women populating these great empires were mothers, fathers, warriors, and healers. They built thriving cities, worshipped their own gods, and kept sacred ceremonies. However, all of this changed when the first Europeans appeared. Men from Spain, called **conquistadors**, arrived in 1519. Shortly after, the ancient civilizations of the Aztecs, the **Maya**, and the Inca were forever changed.

The Aztecs

One of the first civilizations the Spanish encountered was the Aztecs. The Aztec Empire had thrived for thousands of years prior to the Spanish appearance and had formed a sophisticated civilization, complete with chiefs, priests, temples, houses, and deeply rooted religious beliefs. By 1519, the Aztec Empire covered much of present-day Mexico and reached southward as far as today's Guatemala. Several million people inhabited this vast region, all under the Aztec emperor's rule. At the height of Aztec power, the empire's political and cultural center was the grand city of Tenochtitlán. It occupied a swampy island

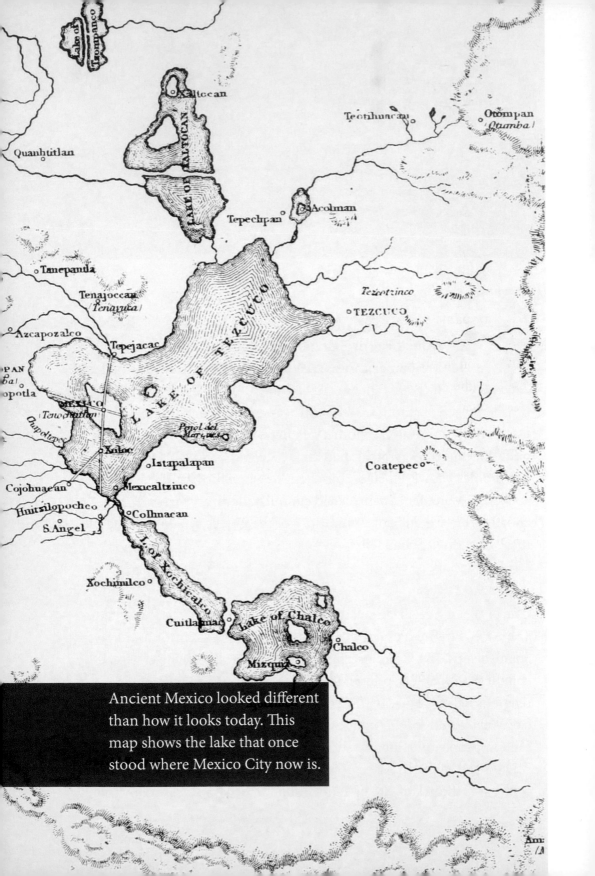

Ancient Mexico looked different than how it looks today. This map shows the lake that once stood where Mexico City now is.

in present-day Mexico's Lake Texcoco. At the time, Tenochtitlán was larger than any city in Europe and one of the largest cities in the world. Where it stood is now Mexico City, the capital of Mexico. According to one account, written by a conquistador, it was a marvel to behold:

> *When we saw so many cities and villages built in the water and other great towns on dry land we were amazed … And some of our soldiers even asked whether the things that we saw were not a dream … seeing things as we did that had never been heard of or seen before, not even dreamed about.*

The Spanish had expected to find a primitive, backward people living in crude villages. Instead, they encountered a highly developed civilization, more advanced than their own in many ways. The sheer scope of the Aztecs' achievements in architecture, agriculture, and science was dazzling.

Who were these gifted people who built such awesome cities? The Aztecs were composed of several ethnic groups who occupied a large part of Mesoamerica, a region extending roughly from what is now central Mexico, down through Nicaragua. Most Aztecs spoke versions of the **Nahuatl** language. This common tongue enabled them to trade with one another throughout the region. The name "Aztec" comes from Aztlán, the legendary birthplace of Nahuatl-speaking peoples.

Ancient History

The mighty Aztec Empire began with a group of people called the Mexica. According to traditional stories, the Mexica embarked on a journey to find a permanent home. Leading them was their patron god, Huitzilopochtli, borne high on a platform. Legend says that the god revealed to them a sign they should seek. He told them that when they saw an eagle perched upon a prickly pear cactus and eating a snake, they were to build their city there.

This drawing shows different styles of dress for Aztec warriors destined to become priests.

Upon reaching Lake Texcoco, the Mexica saw their prophecy fulfilled. There, on an island in the lake, was an eagle posed just as the god had foretold. Upon this island they built their capital city. Assuming a leadership role among neighboring peoples, they adopted the name Anahuac for their domain, to be called "Aztec" in later times.

Researchers have pieced together the Aztecs' history using evidence from archaeological digs, historical records, and language relationships. Nahuatl-speaking people are thought to have originated in the deserts of present-day northern Mexico and the southwestern United States. Around the 1000s or 1100s CE, they began migrating south into the Valley of Mexico, a lake-dotted basin among the mountain ranges of southeastern Mexico. As they drifted, they split into several groups that traveled in different directions—some toward the Pacific Coast, some toward the Gulf of Mexico, and others pushing farther south. Meanwhile, more groups continued to migrate from the north.

One early group, the Toltecs, rose to dominate the region beginning around 900 CE. They established the capital of their **city-state** at Tula, northwest of today's Mexico City. With a population of fifty thousand or more, Tula may have been the largest city in Mesoamerica at the time. The Toltec Empire declined by the late 1100s, however, leaving the region ripe for another takeover as many city-states vied for power.

Soon a new group, the Mexica, migrated into the valley. They arrived at Chapultepec, near Lake Texcoco, around 1248 CE. This was in the powerful city-state of Azcapotzalco, whose ruler allowed the Mexica to build their own city. In 1325, inspired by their vision of an eagle, they built the city of Tenochtitlán on a swampy island in the lake. This fact, at least, intersects with legend. They also elected their first leader, the *tlatoani* or *huey tlatoani*, which means "great speaker." Although the Mexica were under the rule of Azcapotzalco, that arrangement would come to an end.

Two neighboring city-states bordered Tenochtitlán. One was Tlacopan, whose Tepanec people lived on the western bank of Lake Texcoco. The other city-state was Texcoco, whose Acolhua people occupied the lake's northeastern shore. In 1428, the three groups joined to form the Aztec Triple Alliance—to become known as the Aztec Empire. The Aztec Triple Alliance conquered Azcapotzalco, and Itzcoatl, the tlatoani of Tenochtitlán, became the first Aztec emperor.

Under the rule of several emperors, the Aztecs conquered other peoples and expanded their territory over an area stretching from the Pacific Coast to the Gulf of Mexico and south to present-day Guatemala. Although the three city-states were allied, Tenochtitlán became the dominant power and the capital of the empire.

An Empire Is Built

From 1440 to 1469, Itzcoatl's nephew Moctezuma I (also called Montezuma) reigned over the Aztec people. Another nephew, Tlacaelel, worked behind the scenes as chief advisor. Together, the two laid the political and religious foundation of the Aztec Empire.

As the powerful advisor to five successive emperors, Tlacaelel was a major force in raising the status of the Mexica people. He reshaped their traditional beliefs into a religion for all Aztecs. This involved rewriting history as well. To bolster the legitimacy of the Mexica, Tlacaelel promoted the idea that they were descendants of the Toltecs, who were thought of as superior people. He also adopted several gods and religious practices of Teotihuacán, an earlier Mexican empire. When the Aztec Empire conquered new peoples, they destroyed the peoples' religious and historical writings. Once those writings were lost, Aztec emperors could create an "official" history of the Aztec people, weaving into it an empire-wide mythology.

Tenochtitlán's Templo Mayor, or Great Temple, was completed in 1487 and was dedicated to the gods Huitzilopochtli and Tlaloc. Huitzilopochtli, who had been merely the patron god of the Mexica people, was now elevated to Aztec god of the sun and of war. Tlaloc, who had been adopted from the Toltecs, became the god of fertility who brought life-giving rain for crops. Another important Aztec deity was Quetzalcoatl, whose name means "feathered serpent." Mesoamerican peoples had worshiped this god for centuries. When the Aztecs adopted him, he became the god of arts, crafts, and learning.

Many Mesoamerican cultures, including the Toltec, offered sacrifices to their gods. Upon their altars they presented foods, precious goods, animals, and human beings. Under the Aztec Empire, Tlacaelel expanded the practice of human sacrifice. Aztec priests offered thousands of slaves and captured warriors to the gods. They did so to celebrate notable events, but they also believed that this would ensure plentiful crops, stave off natural disasters, and assure that the sun kept moving through the sky.

Aztec Society

Aztec scribes kept records of the empire through lavishly illustrated texts. They recorded government accounts, religious teachings, and histories. From these texts, we learn that Aztec society was ordered

Moctezuma II was a celebrated Aztec leader, and the one such ruler history knows best.

into two general classes, the nobles and the commoners (or peasants). The highest rank among the nobles was the emperor, followed by the high priests and local kings. Commoners, too, were ranked among themselves, from merchants, master craftspeople, and warriors to farmers and slaves.

Aztec rulers did not directly govern the people they defeated. Each conquered city-state usually kept its own tlatoani and ran its own local affairs. These lands became tributary states of the Aztec Empire; that is, they had to pay **tribute**—a kind of tax—in the form of crops, animals, minerals, or goods. Tribute might be payable once or twice a year or as often as every eighty days. Throughout the year, long caravans of tribute bearers made their way to Tenochtitlán.

An Aztec record called the **Codex** Mendoza lists the annual tribute charged to towns in the empire. Some towns provided clothing, such as cloaks, loincloths, and warrior costumes. Others paid tribute in foods, such as bins of maize (corn), beans, fruits, or dried chiles

It was common for Aztec citizens to pay tribute to their leaders.

(chili peppers). Tribute might also take the form of jewelry, such as a quantity of jade necklaces or turquoise medallions. It might be exotic bird feathers, gold, precious stones, seashells, turkeys, deer, or fish. In some cases, tribute was paid in the form of labor, such as when workers were sent to maintain temples and roads. From some places, the tribute consisted of captured warriors. All these payments supported the Aztec emperor and nobles, and they enabled them to build Tenochtitlán into a great city.

The Arrival of the Conquistadors

Into this setting came Hernán Cortés, leader of a Spanish expedition to Mesoamerica. His mission was to take over the region and make it a colony of Spain. Hand-in-hand with this mission were two other goals: to convert the natives to Christianity and to seize as much gold as possible.

Cortés allied himself with the city-state of Tlaxcala, a long-time foe of the Aztec Empire. On November 8, 1519, he and his soldiers entered the capital city of Tenochtitlán. The emperor, Moctezuma II, did not seem to be afraid of this army, in spite of the wonders he observed. The Spaniards' ships were like floating mountains. The Aztecs had never seen guns or horses, so they were amazed at the fire sticks the soldiers carried and the steeds they rode, which seemed like monsters or gigantic deer, with mouths spewing foam like soap suds.

Moctezuma wore grand robes to meet Cortés and offered lavish gifts of gold and other goods. He welcomed the strange newcomers and invited them to live in his palace. Cortés was amazed at Aztec accomplishments. He admired their intelligence and creativity, and he came to respect them. Yet the Spaniards needed to take control of the empire, and they hungered for the Aztecs' gold. Eventually, they took Moctezuma prisoner.

In May 1520, while Cortés was out of Tenochtitlán, his soldiers massacred hundreds of people who had been celebrating a religious festival in the temple. Moctezuma was killed in June, and each side

Hernán Cortés and his army were responsible for nearly extinguishing the Aztec civilization.

blamed the other for his death. The Aztecs drove the Spaniards out of the city. Both sides regrouped for another battle. With their Tlaxcalan allies, the Spaniards marched back to Tenochtitlán, cutting off supply routes. After an eighty-day siege, they wore down the Aztecs completely. In addition to battle fatigue, the Aztec people were weakened by smallpox, introduced by the Spaniards, which swept through the city and took many lives. Emperor Cuauhtémoc surrendered to Cortés on August 13, 1521.

After the conquest, Aztec culture began to decline, and puppet emperors were put in place and controlled by Spanish overlords. The Spaniards destroyed the monumental buildings of Tenochtitlán and built Mexico City on top of the site. Aztec documents were burned, and Christianity replaced the old Aztec beliefs.

Despite the attempt to destroy all traces of the formerly great Aztec Empire, remnants of the empire continue in the modern age. For example, many Mexican towns have Nahuatl names, and more than one million Mexicans still speak the language. Still more are learning to speak the Nahuatl dialect, preserving it for future generations. Other aspects of Aztec culture, such as housing styles, farming methods, and medical techniques, are practiced by some today. Likewise, the most visible sign of the Aztec Empire is the many ruins and treasures that dot the Mexican landscape. These are all signs of one of the greatest lost civilizations in history.

This altar of skulls is part of the ruins of the once great Templo Mayor in Tenochtitlán.

The Structures They Built

P rior to Spanish conquest, the Aztecs had created an impressive culture of great architectural feats. Stone structures, such as temples, houses, and storage buildings, were created and built using skilled craftsmen and slaves. Some of these structures, covered by dense forest over time, continue to be discovered today.

Aztec Architects

When the Mexica people founded Tenochtitlán in 1325, they built a temple to Huitzilopochtli, their patron god, in the center of the island. Beyond the temple **precinct**, the rest of the city was rather unorganized. That began to change when Tenochtitlán became the capital of the Aztec Empire. The population swelled as people left their homes in the countryside to live and work in the bustling capital. Eventually, Tenochtitlán's population grew to more than two hundred thousand people. This influx of residents called for creative urban planning.

Tenochtitlán's architects adopted many features of the empire's other city-state capitals, such as a central plaza. They also incorporated features from the Toltecs' capital city of Tula and the earlier metropolis of Teotihuacán. By drawing on great civilizations of the past, the

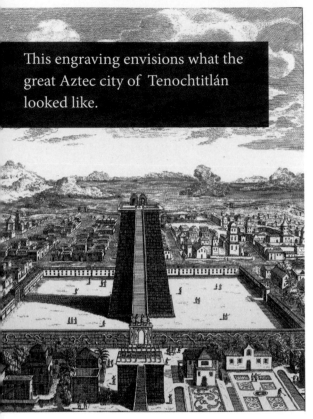

This engraving envisions what the great Aztec city of Tenochtitlán looked like.

Mexica rulers meant to bolster the idea that they were direct descendants of these cultures.

Tenochtitlán's Layout

The heart of the city was the sacred precinct, a plaza enclosed by the elaborately decorated serpent wall. It was lined up along the cardinal directions—north, south, east, and west. Dominating the plaza on the east side was the Templo Mayor, a magnificent temple-pyramid. This massive structure was the tallest building in the city. Nearby was a skull wall, exhibiting row upon row of the skulls of sacrificial victims.

In the center of the plaza was the circular temple of the feathered-serpent god Quetzalcoatl. On the western side was the ball court, where opponents sometimes played for their lives. Dozens of other structures stood within the sacred precinct. They included shrines to various gods; the temple-pyramid of the sun god Tonatiuh; residences for priests; and the *calmecac*, a religious school for the children of nobles. Another building was the Quauhcalli, the headquarters for the elite eagle and jaguar warrior societies, whose members went into battle dressed as their patron animals.

Right outside the sacred precinct was the emperor's lavish palace complex, with courtyards, pools, and gardens. Nearby were the royal zoo, which contained birds and other animals imported from throughout the empire; the house of the *cihuacoatl,* the emperor's chief advisor and second-in-command; and homes of other nobles.

Farther from the city center were shops for merchants and craftspeople and houses for common people. Hundreds of city workers collected garbage and cleaned the streets.

Streets radiated from the city center in four directions, creating a grid pattern and dividing the city into four quarters. Each quarter had a sacred precinct of its own, with a temple, plaza, and city officials' offices. Quarters were further divided into districts or neighborhoods called *calpulli*, each of which had a local temple, school, and chief. Homes and shops were tightly packed along the city streets. Beyond the island's shoreline, hundreds of rectangular garden plots extended the city's boundaries far into the lake.

Designing with Water on the Mind

Tenochtitlán was surrounded by water, so water was a big factor in the city's design. Extending north, west, and south from the island were three **causeways**, or elevated roadways. The western and southern causeways connected the island with the mainland; the northern causeway led to the nearby city of Tlatelolco and farther north. Tlatelolco's market was the largest and busiest in the empire. According to reports from the Spanish, forty thousand to fifty thousand people crowded into the market on each weekly market day.

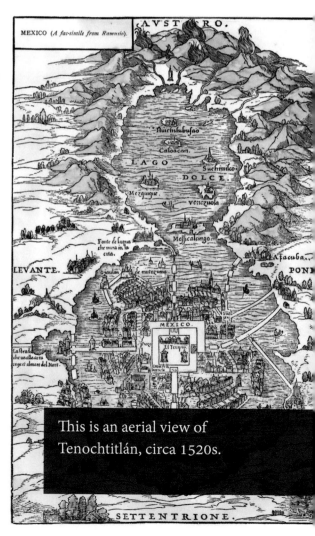

This is an aerial view of Tenochtitlán, circa 1520s.

The causeways were marvels of engineering. They measured about 23 feet (7 meters) wide and 16 feet (5 m) high, standing on earth that had been built up from the lakebed. Here and there were gaps in the causeways where bridges crossed the open water and boats passed underneath. The bridges were moveable so that invaders could not reach the city.

Several of Tenochtitlán's major streets were not roads but canals, where residents traveled in canoes from place to place. This reminded the Spaniards of Venice, Italy, where streets are canals, too. Smaller streets were simply dirt footpaths, and some streets had a footpath and canal side by side. Pedestrians crossed many of the city waterways on wide wooden drawbridges that were raised and lowered.

The waters of Lake Texcoco were brackish, or slightly salty. This water was unsuitable for bathing, cleaning, or drinking. However, freshwater springs bubbled up in the surrounding countryside. Nezahualcoyotl, an expert engineer, designed a double-channeled aqueduct that carried this freshwater into the city from the springs at Chapultepec, on the western mainland. Built in the mid-1400s

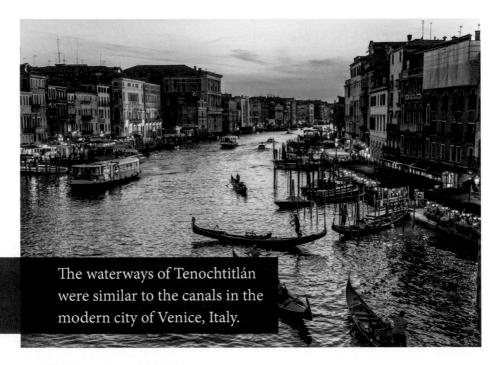

The waterways of Tenochtitlán were similar to the canals in the modern city of Venice, Italy.

with huge terra-cotta walls, the aqueduct was more than 2.5 miles (4 kilometers) long. It ran along the western causeway, rising over the lake to allow for canal traffic.

Transportation

As technologically advanced as the Aztecs were, they were not as advanced in ways of transportation. For instance, they did not use wheeled vehicles. Other prehistoric peoples had been using the wheel for transportation as early as the 3000s BCE. Likewise, the Aztecs did not have large domesticated animals for riding or using as pack animals. Horses and cattle were unknown in the Americas until the Spaniards introduced them. The main modes of travel in the Aztec empire were by foot or canoe.

Large Aztec cities had efficient road systems, and well-worn pathways connected the major cities. These roads were essential to communication as well, and they were well maintained. Beyond the major roadways, though, footpaths could be steep, rocky, muddy, full of holes, or overgrown with tangles of foliage. Long caravans of porters carried goods across the empire on their backs, either bearing tribute to Tenochtitlán or delivering merchant goods to market. Porters often carried heavy loads in a woven reed container like a backpack, supporting it with a strap fastened around the head.

Traveling from place to place was much easier using lakes, rivers, and canals. Aztec canoes glided swiftly through the water, often moving more quickly than a person could walk. Another advantage to using canoes was that they helped carry tremendous loads. Spaniards reported seeing thousands of canoes at a time plying the waters of Lake Texcoco. Aztecs made canoes from the trunks of large trees. They hollowed out the inside of a trunk by carefully burning the wood and then digging it out. Canoes ranged from 14 to 50 feet (4.3 to 15 m) long. A single boatman propelled a canoe using poles or oars. Noblemen cruised in large, flat-bottomed vessels made of wooden pieces lashed together with fibers. Cotton awnings draped overhead shaded them from the sun.

Building Temples

Mesoamerican people had been building temple-pyramids since around 300 BCE. In the Aztec empire, every city-state capital had its own temple-pyramid, oriented so that the sun rose behind it. Unlike the pyramids of ancient Egypt, which were tombs, those in Mesoamerica were temples. Mesoamerican temples were step pyramids, with stone stairways leading to the top. The stairs were so steep that one could not see the top of the structure while standing at its base. This inspired awe as one approached the vicinity of the gods. Instead of coming to a point, these pyramids were flat at the top and crowned with a small temple. High atop this platform, the priests conducted rituals and offered sacrifices. Early Aztec people also began building twin temple-pyramids. These had a double staircase leading upward to a pair of temples, each dedicated to an important god.

This painting shows people building Tenochtitlán.

The site where a temple stood was considered sacred ground, so when a temple was rebuilt, it was not torn down. Instead, the new structure was assembled around and above the old one. Thus, one temple could have several increasingly smaller temples inside it. That was the case with the Templo Mayor in Tenochtitlán, the Aztecs' grandest architectural monument.

After building their first temple in the 1300s, the Aztecs rebuilt it six times over the next 150 years. Building a new temple allowed an

The Templo Mayor

Surely one of the most impressive structures built by the Aztecs was the Templo Mayor. Hernán Cortés described it in this way: "Amongst these temples there is one, the principal one, whose great size and magnificence no human tongue could describe."

The Templo Mayor's rectangular base measured 330 by 260 feet (100 by 80 m)—almost as long as a football field. The major building material was volcanic rock, such as basalt and andesite. Construction workers cut flat slabs, chiseled stair steps, carved statues, and sculpted fierce serpent heads into the stone. As a finishing touch, they coated the whole building with a kind of plaster and multicolored paints. The temple's four sloping sides rose to the upper platform, with a double stairway leading to the top. There stood the shrines of Tlaloc and Huitzilopochtli, with a statue of each god inside.

In spite of his admiration, Cortés destroyed the Templo Mayor and built a Christian cathedral nearby. More than 450 years later, in 1978, city workers in Mexico City who were digging beneath the streets accidentally discovered the remains of the temple. Years of archaeological excavations followed. Today, Mexico City's Museum of the Templo Mayor houses many of the artifacts discovered at the site, and excavations are continuing.

emperor to demonstrate his power, display the city's greatness, and gain favor with the gods. The first temple was a simple structure of earth and wood. Successive temples, each built around the one before, were increasingly decorative. The seventh and final temple, completed around 1487, was a massive structure enclosing all the previous temples. This was the temple the Spaniards saw when they first entered Tenochtitlán. Building it required a remarkable coordination of design, engineering, and construction skills.

Aztecs had not yet begun to use metal tools, so they made sharp cutting tools from hard stone. With these, workers hacked out rock from quarries around Lake Texcoco and carried it to the lakeshore, where canoes loaded and transported it to the building site. There, other workers cut, carved, polished, and assembled the stone parts, creating a glorious ceremonial center for the entire Aztec Empire.

Houses and Homes

The structures that housed ordinary people stood in stark contrast to public buildings. Outside the city-state capitals, homes in rural areas were widely scattered rather than arranged in regular patterns. Resting on stone foundations, they consisted of one- or two-room houses built of **adobe** bricks—a sun-dried mixture of mud and straw—with flat, thatched roofs. Some rural homes were simple huts built of sticks and mud.

The homes of common people who lived in the big cities were much like those of people who lived in rural areas. They were single-story adobe buildings with thatched roofs. Simpler homes had one large open room with four distinct sections. One area was the bedroom, where the whole family slept. Another was the kitchen, and a third was the dining area. The fourth section was a shrine area, where figures of the gods were honored. Finer homes included an adjoining building in which water was heated for residents to take steam baths. This was believed to be a healthful practice.

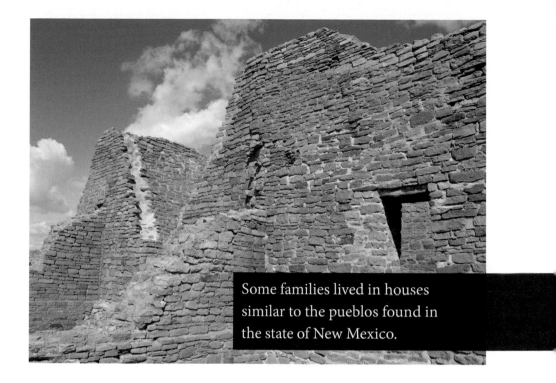

Some families lived in houses similar to the pueblos found in the state of New Mexico.

Those who were more well-to-do lived in homes built around courtyards, in which they prepared food or worked on crafts. In some cases, extended families lived in several houses surrounding a common courtyard. Only high-ranking nobles were allowed to build two-story houses.

The architectural accomplishments of the Aztecs were inspiring. Their ability to create such structures without the help of wheels or large animals testified to the Aztecs' strength as a civilization and as master builders. Their work, although in ruins, has stood the test of time.

¶ Ay vna rayz que sellama. Te-
patli otecpa olotl es pegaxosa como
liga es delamanera dela rayz del
xabon. Es medicinal para las que
braduras de huesos, y tambien v
san della como deliga para tomar
aves, vntan conella pajas lar
gas, y ponen las donde comen
obeuen las aves, y con esto las
toman, tambien llaman aesta
liga tlaçali porque es muy pega
xosa.

¶ Ay otra yerua que sellama
hyiamoli. Enellas sehazen
vnas maçanjtas negras y son
muy amargas son medicina de
la caspa dela cabeça.

Uauhqailtl.

¶Tecpatli, tecpaolotl, caçaltic:
auh çanno iuhquj mamolli, poz
tequjzpatli. Inaqujn mopozteequj
moqujçaloque moquappathoa
icmopepethoa intecpatli: yoa
tlamalonj. tlatlamalonj. ic
maci intotome: çacatitech mo
piloa incanjn imatlian, intla
quaian totome: oncan moma
mana icmahci, icmocaloa: ic
mjtua, motocaiotia: tlahcalli:
cacenca caçaltic yoa icmoça
loa intotome, tototeh mochioa,
caçaliuj. ni tlatecpavia, njtec
pavia, njtlatlaçalhuja.

¶Yiamoli, cafaoac: injqua
uhio pipiaztic, qujltic: injxiuh
io tzotzoltlaca, ixpipitzaoac, ca
capollo, camopaltic, injcacapol
lo: quatequjz iciviz patli inj
cacapollo.

¶Acocotli

petzicatl

Chapter Three

The Aztecs and Farming

A s with all ancient communities, the Aztecs needed a reliable food source in order to survive. At first, they relied on hunting and gathering techniques. Over time, they began to work the land and produce crops. For many Aztecs, agriculture became a necessary way of life.

A Way of Life

Agriculture was the basis of the Aztec economy. The most important crop was maize (corn), which was native to the region. Maize could grow almost anywhere, from the mountainsides to the lowland plains, with diverse varieties flourishing in different areas. It was part of every meal, and Aztec women prepared it in many ways. They ground the kernels into a cornmeal flour, mixed it with water, and cooked it on a hot clay stone to make the flatbreads we still know as tortillas. To make tamales, they formed balls of maize dough, wrapped them in cornhusks, and steamed them in a clay pot. They often placed chiles, beans, or meat inside the tamale. White corn was boiled to produce fat kernels, which were made into a soup called *pozole*.

Nixtamalization of Maize

Before eating maize, the Aztecs put it through a process called **nixtamalization**. This term comes from the Nahuatl word *nixtamalli* a blend of the words for "ashes" and "tamales." Nixtamalization involves soaking and cooking the kernels in a mixture of water and lime (calcium hydroxide) or the ash from burned wood. The kernels swell and soften, and the hulls loosen. This treatment makes the maize tastier, easier to digest, and easier to grind.

The Aztecs probably were not aware of the additional benefits of nixtamalization. It makes maize more nutritious by changing niacin (vitamin B3) into a form that the body can easily absorb. It also kills a deadly fungus that infests corn. The Aztecs did not invent nixtamalization. Mesoamerican people had been using the process since about 1500 BCE, and it is still done today.

Beans were another everyday food for the Aztec people. So was chia, a plant bearing highly nutritious seeds. The Aztecs ate the seeds, made them into a drink, or pressed them to yield oil. They ground seeds from the amaranth plant into flour and prepared it in many of the same ways in which they prepared maize. They would sometimes mold amaranth dough into figurines of the gods, which they would eat on religious holidays. Other Aztec food crops included squash, sweet potatoes, tomatoes, avocados, and many kinds of chiles. The Aztecs also grew cotton, which they wove into cloth for tunics, capes, and other clothing.

Some of the Aztecs' crops were plants that they found growing wild. They would cultivate and care for these plants and raise them for food. Herbs such as cilantro and sage were prized as spices. One of the Aztecs' favorite flavorings came from the pods of the vanilla plant, a member of the orchid family. Another valuable plant was *nopal,* the

Makers of a Chocolate Drink

While the Aztecs were not the originators of the cacao bean or chocolate, they made the cacao bean an important industry in their economy. The cacao bean was first used by the Maya. The Maya began cultivating cacao early in their history, around 900 BCE. From cacao beans they created a cold chocolate beverage, called chocolatl. Only men, and only the noble classes, were allowed to drink the "drink of the gods." The Aztecs eventually also cultivated the cacao bean. They used the precious beans as currency and made offerings of cacao beans to their gods. Cacao trees grew south of Tenochtitlán, so the Aztec emperor demanded from people in the south bags of the beans as tribute. It is thought that either the Aztecs or the Maya introduced the bean to the Spaniards, who popularized it in Europe in the sixteenth century.

Cacao still has important uses in making chocolate drinks and products today.

prickly pear cactus. The broad pads of the cactus and the juicy fruit both are edible, and both are still eaten today. According to modern nutritionists, the Aztecs had an extremely wholesome diet, complete with all the vitamins and minerals required for good health.

Fertilizing and Intercropping

Agriculture was vital to the Aztecs' survival, and they developed highly advanced farming methods. For example, they knew that different crops flourished in different types of soil. They even had different words for sandy soil, rocky soil, firm soil, and so on. Thus they could make good decisions about what to plant in specific areas. They also knew that if they grew just one crop year after year on the same plot of land, the soil lost its nutrients and became infertile. Instead, they practiced **intercropping**—planting crops such as beans or squash between rows of maize. This helped to balance the nutrients in the soil.

The Aztecs also used natural fertilizers to increase the fertility of their farmlands. They mixed rotted plants into the soil, and after

Often, Aztec farmers would plant crops of squash and maize next to each other.

a harvest they buried the plant stalks in the ground. They also used human waste as another common fertilizer. Here and there along the streets and alleyways of Tenochtitlán, huts were placed for use as public toilets. Waste was collected from these huts and sold by the bagful in the marketplace.

Crop Design and Terracing

In the countryside, much of the land was hilly or mountainous. To make the most of this land, the Aztecs used a **terracing** system. They cut terraces, like stair steps, into the hillsides, and they used stone walls or hard soil to hold each level in place. The terraces prevented soil erosion; rainwater could not wash the soil down the hillside. On less steep slopes, the Aztecs held each level of soil in place by planting rows of maguey, also known as agave, or century plants.

The Aztecs devised several irrigation methods to combat droughts and floods that endangered crops. Those who farmed on the level plains dug ditches or canals to collect rainwater for watering their crops. Farmers who lived near a river or lake dug canals to bring water to their land. Some canals were lined with a kind of plaster so that they would last longer.

Because heavy rainfall might flood crops, the Aztecs practiced floodwater irrigation. They built temporary dams on the slopes to capture the floodwaters when it rained heavily. By shifting the dams during a downpour, they could direct the water where it was needed and keep it from flooding the fields.

Chinampas

Tenochtitlán needed tremendous amounts of food crops to support its huge population. Although the emperor demanded foods as tribute from provinces throughout the empire, these food supplies mainly went to his household and those of the priests, other nobles and government officials, and the military. The city-state's thousands of common people needed to raise their own crops to feed themselves.

Farming was a problem in Tenochtitlán. The city was built on a swampy island in a lake. Outside of the imperial city center, most of the island was covered with homes, shops, public buildings, and markets. Where could people raise crops? The answer: in the lake. Beyond the island, the Aztecs constructed huge rectangular garden plots called **chinampas**, which they built up from the bottom of the shallow lakebed. This system of raised fields also was used by the Maya.

Of all the Aztecs' agricultural technology, the chinampa system was the most ingenious. It took many seasons to build up a chinampa. First, farmers drove four long posts into the lakebed, one at each corner of a rectangle, with the posts extending several feet above the water's surface. With the four corners in place, they added reeds along the sides to create upright borders. Next, they wove vines tightly between the reeds to create four "walls" that reached underwater all the way to the lakebed. The garden plot now had a strong, sturdy frame.

The next step was to fill the plot with nutrient-rich material. For this, workers scooped mud from the bottom of the canals. Little by little, they heaped the mud inside the chinampa walls, along with weeds, rotten plants, and soil from the mainland, until the garden's surface stood about 3 feet (1 m) above the lake. They planted trees around the edges for more support.

Chinampas varied in size, but a typical chinampa measured about 100 by 8 feet (30 by 2.5 m). They were built a few feet apart so that the lake waters formed canals between them. *Chinamperos*, or chinampa farmers, paddled their canoes from the mainland and could easily navigate the canals between the gardens. Their crops included maize, beans, squash, chiles, tomatoes, chia, amaranth, and flowers.

At planting time, chinamperos sowed the seeds in beds near the chinampas so they could care for the delicate young plants in their early stage of life. To fertilize the seedlings, they used long-handled baskets to dredge rich mud from the lakebed. When the seedlings were ready for planting, the chinamperos transferred them to the chinampa using a broad-bladed digging stick to make a hole for each seedling.

They arranged the seedlings in long rows with walkways between them. Day after day, throughout the growing season, the farmers rowed out to fertilize and hoe their crops. Finally, at harvest time, they loaded the plants onto their canoes and rowed to land-based markets.

Chinampas formed a ring around the island of Tenochtitlán. However, these gardens did not produce enough food for the city's enormous population. Much more chinampa farming took place on the nearby lakes of Xochimilco and Chalco. These ancient lakes no longer exist; they have been filled in to create more dry land for settlement. In the Aztecs' time, however, they were part of a chain of lakes in the Valley of Mexico. They lay south of Tenochtitlán and were connected by a narrow water channel to Lake Texcoco. With more than 22,000 acres (8,900 hectares) of farmland, Lake Xochimilco's chinampas provided food for tens of thousands of people. Farmers there grew both vegetables and flowers.

The chinampa system of farming continues today in Mexico.

Chinamperos and their families did not own the chinampas they farmed. The gardens belonged to the emperor or his nobles. The job of managing the gardens fell to the *calpulli*—the local district or neighborhood. Each farmer was assigned a certain number of chinampas to cultivate. If he failed to farm a chinampa for three years in a row, it was taken from him. This is why crop rotation was so important. If the soil in one chinampa was wearing out, its farmer could plant a different crop to restore the soil and keep his right to farm there.

Chinampas in Xochimilco

Today, Mexico City's southern borough of Xochimilco stands where Lake Xochimilco was under the Aztec Empire. Flowers were an important crop—the name Xochimilco comes from the Nahuatl word for "flower garden place." Today, some of the ancient chinampas have been converted to huge flower gardens, with canals weaving among them. Colorful, flat-bottomed boats called *trajineras* take visitors on cruises through the canals. Xochimilco has fewer chinampas now because the water level of the lake has dropped, and many areas have been built over. In less visited areas of the city, however, farmers still raise corn, spinach, lettuce, and other vegetables on their chinampas.

Spaniards were amazed when they saw the Aztecs' chinampa system. They wrote romantic accounts of the chinampas, calling them "floating gardens." They were actually artificial islands, firmly anchored to the lakebed. Chinampa farming was highly productive, with 1 acre (0.4 hectares) of land yielding several tons of maize. The chinampa system is still practiced today in some parts of

Spinach grows in a field by the canals of Lake Xochimilco today.

Mexico, where productivity equals or even exceeds that of farming with modern, high-tech systems.

It is clear the Aztecs developed sophisticated ways of farming to ensure their livelihoods. Their techniques had been practiced and passed down over generations. Today, other cultures use similar farming techniques, such as terracing and intercropping, unknowingly continuing the legacy of the Aztecs.

This drawing features Acamapichtli, the first Aztec king.

Chapter Four

Masters of Text

In addition to designing and building impressive structures and farming, the Aztecs developed ways of recording events, memories, and daily happenings. They had people dedicated to writing everything down, and others devoted to making the scrolls on which these records were written. Paper, books, and writing were integral parts of preserving and perpetuating Aztec culture.

Making Paper

Outside the sacred precinct of Tenochtitlán, beyond the nobles' palaces, stood the homes of papermakers. The material they produced was of vital importance in conducting the business of the empire. Scribes recorded information by painting descriptive pictures on paper. This intricately detailed writing system was capable of expressing very complex concepts. Some records were inscribed on cloth, deerskin parchment, or paper made from leaves of the maguey plant. However, the most common paper in the empire was *amatl* (*amate* in Spanish).

Mexico's Maya people were making paper as early as the 400s CE. The craft eventually spread to other Mesoamerican peoples. Aztec papermakers adopted their techniques and improved upon them. They made amatl from the inner bark of the wild fig tree, first stripping off the stringy bark fiber with a knife and then soaking it in water. Then they boiled the fibers and laid them on a wooden board to dry. Next, they pounded the fibers to soften them and make them cling together. The hammer for pounding paper, called a bark beater, was a grooved basalt stone with a wooden handle. They pounded the fibers until they became a thin, flat, brownish sheet. The papermakers then trimmed the sheets, polished them, and applied a thin film of plaster to create a smooth painting surface.

Some paper was made in Tenochtitlán, but the empire procured most of its paper through tributes from outlying areas. A tribute chart for the emperor Moctezuma II reads "Twenty-four thousand resmas of paper are to be brought yearly to the storehouses of the ruler of Tenochtitlán." A *resma*, or ream, was a bundle of twenty sheets. So 24,000 resmas would add up to the staggering quantity of 480,000 sheets of paper paid every year as tribute.

Most paper came from the region of Morelos, now a state south of Mexico City. Many varieties of fig grew there, and papermaking was the regional specialty. Sheet sizes probably differed, but one village's paper sheets measured 18 by 13.5 inches (46 by 34 centimeters).

At tribute time, long lines of paper bearers set off for Tenochtitlán. They did not use wheeled carts or pack animals, so humans bore the load. Over mountains, through rivers, and across the plains they trekked, finally arriving at the southern causeway into the capital city. The finest, whitest paper went to the priests and other high officials. Lower-quality paper in oddly shaped pieces ended up in the marketplace, where common people could buy it.

Paper had a variety of uses in Aztec life. Some was made into ceremonial clothing to be worn for religious rituals. Capes and headdresses might be decorated with paper bows and other ornaments. People might carry paper flowers or wear paper earrings. It was sometimes used as an offering to the gods. Statues of the gods might be adorned with paper, too. It also played a role in funeral ceremonies:

The Codex Mendoza

The Codex Mendoza is an Aztec book created for the New Viceroy of Spain, Antonio de Mendoza, around 1541. While under Spanish rule, the Aztec codex writers were instructed to create these richly decorated books that detailed the lifestyle and daily happenings of the Aztec peoples. This included information on the rulers of the Aztecs, yearly tribute, religious beliefs and practices, and ceremonies celebrated at different times in an Aztec's life.

The Codex Mendoza was eventually put on a ship headed to Spain, where it would make its way to the Holy Roman emperor, Charles V. However, along the way, the ship was attacked by French privateers, and the codex was stolen. It eventually ended up in an Englishman's collection, and today it resides in the Bodleian Library in Oxford, England.

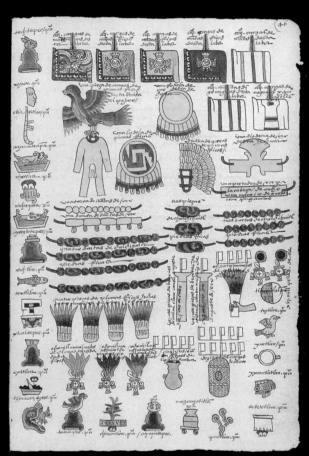

A scene in the Codex Mendoza

Several bits of paper were placed with a body before it was burned or buried. Each piece was a kind of passport or token of safe passage to carry the deceased safely through the journey in the afterlife. The major use of paper for the Aztecs, however, was in making codices (the plural form of "codex").

Books

Codices were Aztec books. A codex began as a strip of paper many feet long, either a single sheet or smaller sheets joined together. The strip was folded like an accordion, with zigzag creases, into a thick bundle that could be opened to any page. Both sides of the paper were painted so that one could read the "book" on both sides. The Maya people had a similar process for making codices.

Only a few codices survive from the period before the Spanish conquest of 1521. Aztecs continued to make codices afterwards. The Spaniards taught the Aztecs to record their Nahuatl language in Western script, and they also schooled them in Spanish and

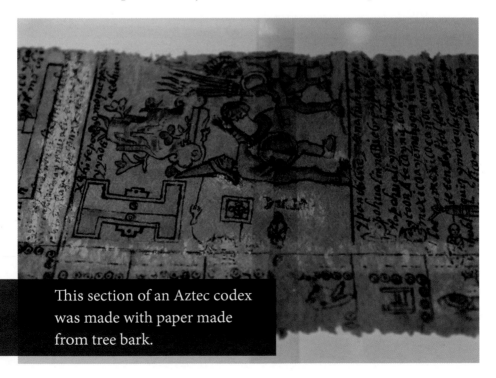

This section of an Aztec codex was made with paper made from tree bark.

Latin. Thus, many of the post-conquest codices include not only traditional Aztec pictures but also written inscriptions in Nahuatl, Spanish, and sometimes Latin. About five hundred codices still exist, each with a name, such as Codex Mendoza, Codex Borgia, Florentine Codex, and so on.

Some codices were historical records. They listed each year in an emperor's reign and recorded all the events that happened that year. Others were religious books. They portrayed the gods and their powers, illustrated the days of the religious calendar, and depicted rituals to be performed on each occasion. Another type of codex was administrative. It recorded official government information such as tribute lists, landholdings, or maps of the empire's city-states.

The scribes who produced these books were professional artists called *tlacuilos*. They were specially trained not only in writing, drawing, and painting, but also in Aztec religious symbolism. The scribes used charcoal for the color black to sketch outlines. For other colors, they ground minerals and plants and dissolved them in water to create red, green, blue, and yellow paints. Scribes held an honored position in Aztec society. Some priests and nobles were scribes themselves, but many scribes were commoners working under a master's direction. The position of scribe was sometimes passed down from father to son, and each scribe specialized in making one type of codex.

Writing Aztec History

The Aztec writing system used pictures instead of words to convey information. Some of these pictures were simple pictograms. That is, they depicted common objects such as a cactus, a stone, or an ear of corn. Anyone could understand pictograms, regardless of his or her native language. Other pictures are **glyphs**, which is short for "hieroglyphs." Like Egyptian hieroglyphics, glyphs represent words, sounds, or ideas.

This *tzompantli*, or skull rack, appears in the ruins of the Templo Mayor in Mexico City.

Some glyphs are fairly simple. They represent an idea that is easy to interpret. For example, a pyramid in flames represents the conquest of a city. A trail of footprints stands for walking, motion, or a sequence of events. Other glyphs combine pictures of well-known objects. For example, a hill with a jaguar's head on top stands for a place called Ocelotepec. This town was on a hilltop where jaguars live. Its name combines the words *ocelot* ("jaguar") and *tepec* ("hill").

Many glyphs are tricky to decipher because of the way they combine words, objects, and concepts. For example, some Aztec place names end with *-tlan*. That suffix means "place abundant with." At the same time, *tlan* is part of the Nahuatl word *tlantli*, which means "teeth." Thus, a picture of an object plus a set of teeth stands for a town that has a lot of that object. The glyph for the town of Coatlan is a snake with teeth below it. This combines *coatl* ("snake") with *-tlan* to indicate the place with many snakes.

Even more difficult to understand are glyphs that combine Nahuatl word fragments to represent another word. As an example, the town of Mapachtepec means "hill of the raccoon." Naturally, the bottom of its glyph is a hill (tepec). The top, however is not a *mapach*, or raccoon. Instead, it is a hand (*maitl*) and a chunk of moss (*pachtli*). By combining *ma-* from maitl and *-pach* from pachtli, we get mapach— the raccoon. No one knows how or why the Aztecs developed such a complex writing system. However, it enabled them to record an incredible amount of information in great detail.

Today, historians use the Aztec codices to help understand the Aztec's history and rituals. They are especially useful to excavation teams exploring the Aztec's buried cities. For example, several codices depict human sacrifices and certain sacrificial practices. In 2015, a team working in the Templo Mayor discovered a room full of decapitated skeletal heads, all mortared together on large poles, as a sort of rack, and all facing inward. This was what the codices refer to as *tzompantli*, or a type of trophy skull rack. This was the first instance of a mortared tzompantli ever discovered, and the first time the skulls were seen arranged in a circle, all looking inward—at what remains unknown. Nevertheless, from this discovery, it is clear that the Aztecs' written language and practices still hold relevance today.

The Aztecs made calculations and predictions based on the movements and positionings of stars and planets.

The Legacy of the Aztecs

The Aztecs were expert mathematicians and astronomers, and surprisingly, had an incredible ability to calculate huge sums—as far as into the millions. Their concept of time—seasons, months, and years—was also strikingly similar to our modern ways of thinking. Finally, the ability to tend ailments and injuries with herbs and other medical techniques also fashioned them into accomplished healers. All of these achievements have helped the Aztecs leave a legacy on the history of their people and the world.

Understanding Numbers

The Aztecs had one of the most advanced mathematics systems in the ancient world. They could compute figures so large that we need calculators to handle them today. Besides addition and subtraction, they were able to do multiplication and division. Using a type of geometry, they accurately calculated the areas of fields, even if they had irregular shapes.

The Aztecs also needed mathematics for the complex accounting system they used to keep track of the tribute each city paid. Their written records show hundreds of pages of these lists. The symbol for a city is followed by the symbol for goods, such as maize, and the symbol for the quantity.

To understand Aztec numbers, let's start with our own numbering system. We use a base-10 system, with the number 10 as the basic unit. We build numbers using multiples of 10: $1 \times 10 = 10$; $10 \times 10 = 100$; $10 \times 10 \times 10 = 1,000$; and so on. The Aztecs used a base-20 system, with 20 as the basic building block. As in their writing system, they represented numbers with signs and pictures. Numbers from 1 through 19 were shown as dots or sometimes as pictures of fingers. A flag, or sometimes a shell or a vase of grass, stood for the number 20. For example, three flags would mean the number 60. A feather-like figure signified 400 (20×20). A bag or pouch meant 8,000 ($20 \times 20 \times 20$) because it stood for a standard bag of 8,000 cacao beans.

Understanding the Stars

For the Aztecs, astronomy was closely linked to mathematics, the calendar, religious practices, and temple architecture. To them, astronomy and **astrology** were the same. The heavenly bodies represented gods who held the fate of humans in their hands. They believed that it was vitally important to study the stars to discern the gods' moods and take the necessary course of action.

The empire's astronomers were priests and nobles. They observed the skies from locations within a temple or on rooftops. They noted the movements of the sun, moon, planets, stars, and constellations. Where and when the sun rose was especially important. Astronomers tracked these locations by viewing the objects along a wooden stick with crossbars set across the sight line. What they found determined when certain rituals should be performed and when particular gods should be honored.

Astronomy was also used to determine the orientation of a temple—that is, what direction it faced. The Templo Mayor in Tenochtitlán, for example, faced west. It is believed to have been built

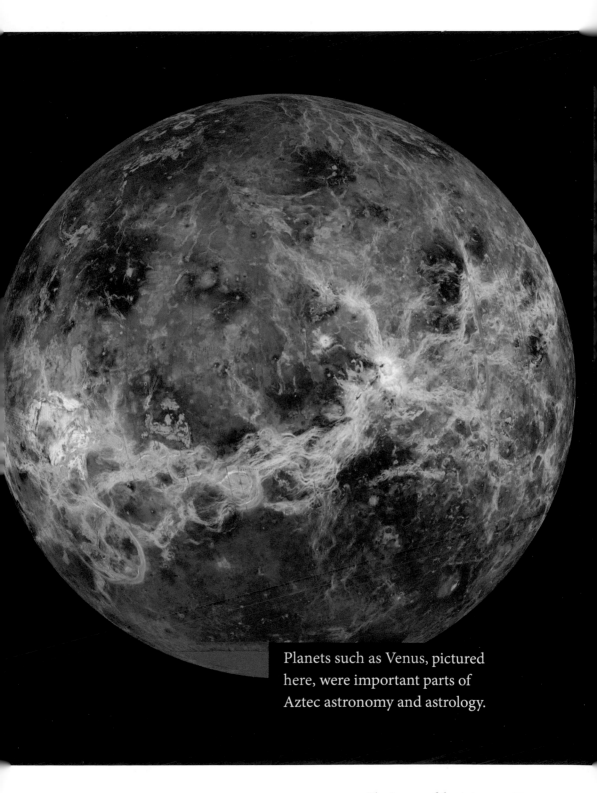

Planets such as Venus, pictured here, were important parts of Aztec astronomy and astrology.

so that on the spring **equinox**, March 21, the sun rose directly between the double temples of Huitzilopochtli and Tlaloc.

Aztec astronomers also tracked the orbit of the planet Venus, which they dreaded as an ominous force. In the course of its orbit, Venus first rises as a morning star, then disappears, then rises again as an evening star. Since Venus rises before the sun, the Aztec people saw it as immensely powerful, embroiled in a fierce battle between the forces of night and day. The Aztecs correctly measured Venus's cycle around the sun at 584 days, and the empire's astronomers could predict its movements. An ancient Aztec record foretells the cycles of Venus over 104 years. That is the span of time it takes for Venus's orbit and the two Aztec calendars to coincide. A whole series of mystical number relationships were built around this.

Understanding Time

The Aztecs organized their days according to two different calendars. Both required a firm grasp of mathematics. The *tonalpohualli* (meaning "day count") was a religious calendar. Priests used it to forecast the future, to determine which gods held power at various times, and to learn when opposing deities were clashing. One day may be a good time to wage battle, but another day may bring sickness. Yet another day may call for rituals to ward off a looming danger. Priests also used this calendar to draw up the horoscope of an emperor or nobleman or to tell the fortune of a newborn child.

The elaborate religious calendar was a 260-day cycle organized into twenty groups of thirteen days each. (Spaniards called the thirteen-day "weeks" *trecenas*.) Each day was designated both by a number and a day name. Twenty day names were each represented by a symbol, beginning with Crocodile and Wind and ending with Rain and Flower. Each symbol was associated with a god and with one of the cardinal directions (north, south, east, and west).

To go through the cycle, Aztecs matched the numbers 1 through 13 with symbols 1 through 20. For example, the first day was

1 Crocodile, the second day was 2 Wind, and so on. The fourteenth day began with the number 1 again but continued with the fourteenth symbol. After reaching the twentieth symbol on day 7 Flower, the symbols started over, so the next day was 8 Crocodile. This way, each day had a unique combination of a number plus a symbol. In 260 days the cycle returned to the beginning—1 Crocodile.

The other Aztec calendar, *xiuhpohualli* (meaning "year count"), was a solar calendar, based on the sun's position throughout the year. Similar to our Gregorian calendar, it had 365 days, but the days were arranged in eighteen months of twenty days each. The five extra days at the end of the year were considered unlucky. These "empty days" were a time of uncertainty, when people fasted, took part in cleansing rituals, and hoped the sun would return in the new year.

Today, because a solar year is actually one-fourth of a day longer than 365 days, we add an extra day every four years. It is not clear how the Aztecs dealt with leap years. Some scholars believe that the Aztecs began each new year at a different time of day: One year began at midnight, the next year began in the early morning, the next at midday, and the next in the evening. This added one-fourth of a day to every year, for a total of one complete day every four years.

The Aztecs' solar calendar marked the seasons and years as we know them. They used it to determine when to hold monthly ceremonies and when to perform rituals related to the seasons. For this reason, it was probably related to the cycle of agricultural activities. The calendar also organized everyday life, just as our own calendar organizes our days, weeks, and months. Every twenty-day month was divided into four weeks of five days each. Thus, weekly events such as market day took place every five days.

Years were given names, too. That is how we can tell what year an event took place in the Aztecs' historical records. As with the religious calendar, each year had a number and a picture symbol, matched according to a complex system. Year 13 Acatl (13 Reed), for example, is believed to be 1479, the year the Sun Stone was carved. To distinguish

Officially known as the Sun Stone, scientists believe the Aztec calendar actually reflects the Aztec people's view of the universe rather than a record of dates. It depicts the cycles of creation and destruction throughout eons of time.

Before the present time, according to Aztec mythology, there were four eras called suns, each ruled by a sun god. One after the other, each sun god perished, and a new god began his reign. The present era—the last one—is known as the Fifth Sun. It is ruled by the sun god Tonatiuh, whose name means "He Who Goes Forth Shining." While previous sun gods had been still, Tonatiuh was the first to move through the sky. Thus, he required a constant stream of sacrificial victims to assure that he would continue to rise.

Carved from basalt rock around 1479, the 25-ton (22.7-metric-ton) Sun Stone measures about 12 feet across by 4 feet thick (3.7 by 1.2 m). At the center is the ghastly face of Tonatiuh. Around his head are four panels representing the downfall of the four previous suns who perished by jaguars, winds, fiery rain, and floods. Beyond them, a circular band depicts the twenty day-signs of the religious calendar. Eight triangles represent both rays of the sun and pointers toward the directions. Two fire serpents meet face to face on the outer rim, and gods of day and night emerge from their mouths.

Workers dug up the Sun Stone in the Zócalo, Mexico City's central plaza, in 1790. It is now displayed in the city's National Museum of Anthropology.

A reproduction of the Aztec Sun Stone

A dancer in Aztec dress lights a torch at a ceremony in 2015.

year names from day names, a year name was often enclosed in a rectangular box.

Once every fifty-two years, the first day of the Aztecs' two calendars fell on the same day. The entire fifty-two–year cycle was known as the calendar round. It was represented in pictures as a bundle of fifty-two reeds, indicating a "bundle" of years. This day was the occasion for the New Fire Ceremony, when the fate of humankind was uncertain, hanging between life and death.

In preparation, the Aztecs put out all fires throughout the empire. In the middle of the night, priests stood atop a mountain peak near Tenochtitlán and offered sacrifices. Meanwhile, people stood on their rooftops awaiting the outcome. At last, the priests lit a new flame and built a huge bonfire. Men from all corners of the empire lit their torches from this fire and carried the new flame back to their villages. If the ceremony went as planned, it assured that the sun would rise the next morning to begin a new fifty-two-year cycle. If the ceremony failed—say, if the new fire did not light properly—the world would plunge into darkness and monsters would devour the Earth.

Understanding Plants and Medicine

Aztec doctors had a vast knowledge of **botany**, the study of plants, and they relied heavily on herbal cures. The emperor Moctezuma I even established a botanical garden in Huaxtepec, in today's state of Morelos. It was a sort of plant museum containing hundreds of species. As he conquered new territories, he had their native plants brought to his garden. Moctezuma ordered his doctors to conduct medical research using various herbs to see which ones helped to cure specific illnesses.

The Spaniards marveled at the emperor's garden. No such institution existed in Europe. They noted that the Aztecs used substantially more medicinal plants than Europeans did. According to one Spanish missionary, "They have their own native skilled doctors who know how to use many herbs and medicines … Some of them have so much experience that they were able to heal Spaniards, who had long suffered from chronic and serious diseases."

The Aztecs believed in three basic causes of illnesses. Supernatural causes had to do with astronomical conditions, a person's individual horoscope, or punishments from the gods. Magical causes resulted from

Plants and herbs became important elements of Aztec medicine.

The Aztecs used the agave, or maguey, plant to treat injuries.

a curse or a spell cast upon a patient. Some disorders were due merely to natural causes. Doctors used herbal medicines to treat everything from pimples and headaches to chest pains and epilepsy. They also developed remedies for fear, timidity, stupidity, and a mind unbalanced by a tornado. With the Aztecs' unique cultural approach to medicine, many of their cures were remarkably effective.

Fortunately, a few codices survive with Aztec medical information, complete with colorful plant illustrations. These books contain a wealth of expert knowledge about natural substances for treating diseases. The Badianus Codex, for example, illustrates more than two hundred herbs and includes descriptions of what ailments they cure.

Aztec doctors had names for hundreds of herbs, roots, barks, and other plant substances. In many cases, modern scientists have figured out which plants the Aztecs refer to, although some are still known only by their Nahuatl names. Each substance had a specific use in treating a disease, illness, or injury. For example, juice from the prickly pear cactus was used to reduce swelling. The maguey, or agave, plant was used to treat wounds. The extract from a balsam tree relieved blisters and toothaches. Some of these treatments are still in use today.

Researchers are finding that ancient herbal medicines may offer cures that modern scientists have been seeking for decades. For this reason, the Aztec medical codices could be immensely important to medical science. Scientists today are testing many of the Aztec medicines to learn more about their healing properties. After centuries of neglect, the Aztecs' ancient cures may unlock some of the medical mysteries of the twenty-first century.

Despite the great Aztec Empire and peoples disappearing from the world centuries ago, the traces they left behind—buildings, books, and medical insights—continue to influence and intrigue modern historians, scientists, and doctors. Their achievements made them one of the most technologically advanced societies the world has ever known. Their legacy will live on for centuries to come.

Chronology

circa 300 BCE Mesoamerican people are building early
temple-pyramids.

400s CE Mexico's Maya people are making paper for books.

1000s–1100s Nahuatl-speaking people begin migrating south
through Mexico.

ca. 1100 The Mexica people begin their southward migrations.

ca. 1248 Mexica people settle in Chapultepec, west of Lake Texcoco.

1325 The Mexica establish Tenochtitlán on an island in Lake Texcoco.

1428 The Aztec Empire is established when Tenochtitlán, Tlacopan, and
Texcoco form the Triple Alliance.

1430s The emperor Itzcoatl enhances Tenochtitlán by building temples,
roads, and a causeway, and institutes the tribute system.

mid-1400s Under Moctezuma I, Nezahualcoyotl of Texcoco builds an
aqueduct to bring water from the mainland to Tenochtitlán.

1473 Tenochtitlán takes over its northern sister city of Tlatelolco, which
becomes the Aztecs' largest marketplace.

ca. 1479 The massive Aztec Sun Stone is carved in Tenochtitlán.

1487 The Templo Mayor is completed, including a wall around the sacred precinct.

1507 Moctezuma II holds the Aztecs' last New Fire Ceremony at the end of a fifty-two–year cycle.

1521 Spanish conquistador Hernán Cortés conquers the Aztec Empire.

1541 The Codex Mendoza is written.

1552 Aztec doctor Martin de la Cruz writes the Badianus Codex, a manual on herbs and their medicinal uses.

1831 The Codex Mendoza is placed in the Bodleian Library in Oxford, England.

1914 Excavations at the Templo Mayor begin.

2015 Excavators in the Templo Mayor discover a *tzompantli*, or a skull trophy rack.

Glossary

adobe A type of brick or a wall made of a sun-dried mixture of mud and straw.

astrology The practice of studying heavenly bodies to determine conditions and events in human affairs.

botany The study of plants.

causeway An elevated roadway over a body of water.

chinampa A raised garden bed built up in a swamp or lakebed.

city-state An administrative area comprising a city and its surrounding territory.

codex (plural **codices**) A book with turning pages, as opposed to a scroll; Aztec codices were long sheets of paper folded like an accordion into a compact form.

conquistador A Spanish soldier sent to conquer lands in the Americas.

equinox One of two days during the year when day and night have equal lengths; the spring equinox is around March 21; the autumn equinox is around September 22.

glyph Short for "hieroglyph;" picture writing in which the pictures represent words, sounds, or ideas.

intercropping The practice of planting rows of crops that enrich the soil between rows of crops that remove nutrients from the soil.

Maya A civilization that flourished in Mexico's Yucatán Peninsula, southeast of Aztec territory, from about 1500 BCE until the Spaniards arrived in the 1500s CE.

Mesoamerica The region of southern North America occupied by the Aztecs before the arrival of the Spanish in the 1500s.

Nahuatl The language spoken by the Aztecs.

nixtamalization A process of soaking and cooking maize kernels to soften them.

precinct A disctrict or region.

terracing A system for farming on hillsides by cutting the soil in a steplike pattern, creating many levels for planting.

tribute Regular payment made to a ruler, sometimes in the form of goods.

Further Information

Books

Apte, Sunita. *The Aztec Empire*. True Books. New York: Scholastic, 2010.

Ganeri, Anita. *How the Aztecs Lived*. Life in Ancient Times. New York: Gareth Stevens, 2011.

Green, Jen. *Aztecs*. Flashback History. New York: PowerKids Press, 2010.

Levy, Buddy. *Conquistador: Hernán Cortés, King Montezuma, and the Last Stand of the Aztecs*. New York: Bantam Books, 2009.

MacDonald, Fiona. *You Wouldn't Want to Be an Aztec Sacrifice!* New York: Scholastic, 2013.

Raum, Elizabeth. *The Aztec Empire: An Interactive History Adventure*. You Choose: Historical Eras. Mankato, MN: Capstone Press, 2012.

Webb, Christine, ed. *Eyewitness Aztec*. New York: DK Publishers, 2011.

Websites

DK Find Out: The Aztecs

http://www.dkfindout.com/us/history/aztecs

Learn all about the Aztecs at this interactive, illustrated timeline.

Ducksters: Aztec Empire

http://www.ducksters.com/history/aztec_empire/daily_life.php

Understand more about how the Aztecs lived at this website.

KidsKonnect: Ancient Aztec Facts

http://www.kidskonnect.com/history/ancient-aztec

Read about the Aztecs and the important parts of their culture at this website.

KidsPast: The Aztecs

http://www.kidspast.com/world-history/0281-aztecs.php

Discover the history of the Aztecs and what led to the fall of the Aztec empire here.

Mr. Donn: Aztecs

http://www.aztecs.mrdonn.org

Explore more about the Aztecs and their great civilization at this website.

Index

Page numbers in **boldface** are illustrations. Entries in **boldface** are glossary terms.